Everyone can learn to ride a bicycle

Chris Raschka

schwartz & wade books · new york

To Anne and Lee

Visit us on the Web! randomhouse.com/kids

Educators and librarians, for a variety of teaching tools,
visit us at RHTeachersLibrarians.com

Library of Congress Cataloging-in-Publication Data
Raschka, Christopher.
Everyone can learn to ride a bicycle / Chris Raschka.
— 1st ed.
p. cm.
Summary: A father teaches his daughter all about bicycle riding,
from selecting the right bike to trying again after a fall.
ISBN 978-0-375-87007-1 (hardcover)
ISBN 978-0-375-97007-8 (lib. bdg.)
[1. Bicycles and bicycling—Fiction. 2. Fathers and daughters—
Fiction.] I. Title. PZ7.R1814Eve 2013
[E]—dc23   2012009172

The text of this book is set in Bodoni Old Face.
The illustrations were rendered in ink and watercolor.

MANUFACTURED IN CHINA

10 9 8 7 6 5 4 3 2 1

First Edition

Want to learn to ride a bicycle?

First you need

to choose

the perfect bike for you.

Let's go!

Watch
everyone
ride.

They all learned how.

Come on, let's give it a try.

Training wheels are helpful.

They keep you from tipping over.

If we raise them up a smidge,

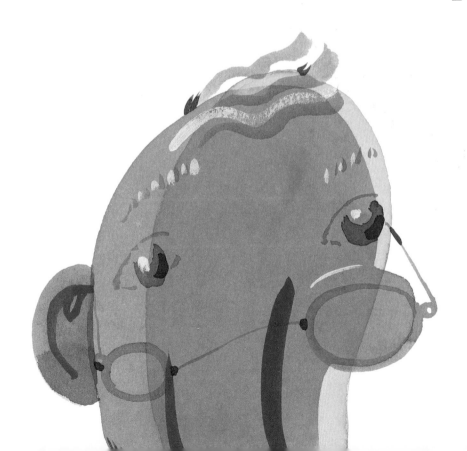

you'll begin to feel your balance.

Now we take them off.

That's a bit scary,

but try it

in the grass.

Too hard to pedal.

Maybe down a small hill?

Oh dear.

I'll hold on.

Pump your legs!

Oops!

You nearly had it.

Don't give up.

You'll get it.

Find the courage

to try it again,

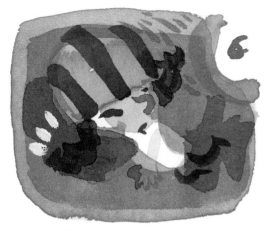

again,

and again,

and again,

again,

and again,

and again,

until

by luck,

grace,

and determination,

you are riding

a bicycle!

(And now you'll never forget how.)